As Thyself By Nia

Nia Jovan Andrews

Published by: Jones Publishing & Enterprises, LLC.
(JP&E LLC)

Registered Offices: 515 North State Street Chicago, Illinois

JP&E and the open book are identifying marks of Jones Publishing & Enterprises, LLC

Dedication

I am so grateful to be able to complete this memoir. I can remember when I was a little girl and I first learned to read. I would come home from kindergarten every day to teach my grandfather what I learned. My grandfather was from the south (Mississippi) and never learned to read. So, I was on a mission to help him. Unfortunately, he died February 1991 and I never got the chance to fully teach him; he used to fall asleep through our teach-ing sessions too, so that made the learning process take a bit longer. But, granddaddy meant the world to me. Granddaddy, I named my publishing company to hon-or you and I am not done yet. You could not read, but I write, publish and distribute books. Thank you for being a protector that loved your girls.

Robert Magic "Boots" Jones

Table of Contents

Introduction

Feeling alone, rejected and abandoned is not a place anyone wants to be, especially in their twenties. For me, even more, when I've worked so hard to please everyone around me. I started working when I was told, when I did that I successfully met sales goals, then was promoted. I bought everything I wanted without having to ask, beg, or plead. I provided for my munchkin (Daniel Jr.). I did not have to lay on the altar of sin by sacrificing my body or talents for a man or anyone to take care of us. I had help from my mother and other family members, but the majority of the responsibility for caring for him was on me. I did it too. I made sure anywhere he went he was a representation of what I was capable of doing for him. If that meant name brands, he had it.

My agenda was to please people. I knew how important it was to make everyone around me happy. I felt the pressure of the expectations that people had on my life. At 19-years-old, I learned of this expectation when I began to tell people after six-months of hiding it that I was pregnant. I worked in a bank and I told my coworker, and her response was, "but Nia you're so much smarter than that." I did not know what that meant at the time, but I learned it meant that we see you as the one who will set the bar higher.

For many people, I was the one who would chase my dreams. This seemed to be the forecast over my life, but I was clueless to it. I was the girl that the thugs pro-tected, when I was in the wrong place at the wrong time they would say, no not her. I was the one who they never passed the blunt to. I was the one who was never asked for sexual escapades. In my immaturity, I did not understand why. I thought maybe I was not cool enough. It seemed people thought I should be the "lame." I did not rebel against that though, I embraced it. I liked the respect that came with it. I saw that it caused people to admire me. It went to my head. I finished school, while working, but living life how I thought I wanted to. I did not count-up the time I was wasting, I did not consider that the perception that I was clueless to was really in God's plan for my life; I was too young and too full of myself to see that. Everyone seemed to take it seriously, but me. I either did not see it at all, or saw it so much where it made me haughty and self-righteous.

By the time I was 25 years old, I needed a balance. I needed stable ground. I was tired of feeling shunned from what was popular, while expected to always do the right thing, but then I was tired of being a people pleaser too. I know this does not seem like a huge problem, seeing that people feel lost for reasons like abuse, molestation, rape and many other tragedies. I am not that girl though. I do not have that story. I am an average girl who was trying to find her way through all the confusion that life placed in front of me. By the time I was twenty-five, I felt like life had been this room full of ropes from floor to ceiling filling it and I was pulling through them trying to find my way out. I was trying to find my purpose, trying to figure out what people saw in me that I did not see in myself, why was I a mother, a mother like for real a mom. That made me even question if there was a God, because in my mind, nothing or no one in their right mind would give me that responsibility, not as lost as I was.

All of the questions and anxiety to figure it out built-up. I did not know where to turn for the answers. Everyday, I grew more and more frustrated, because I felt clueless.

With that, I felt responsible. I felt like I had these answers. As if, I held the answers to what I was seeking, but I did not know how to find it. I turned to working, feeling puffed-up in my education, sex in relationships, shopping and ego. None of that satisfied my desire. When none of these things made me happy, I abused relationships by using them only for when they worked for me and when I was not feeling them I walked away, carelessly. I spent time in the company of people who were just as lost as I was. I felt hopeless and still I could not see nor understand how or why people saw what they saw in me.

That's how I was feeling on the inside. On the outside, I was still maintaining the things and holding-up. However, the time came when I began to lose those things, because I just stopped caring. I gave-up on jobs, I lost cars, I abandoned relationships how I was feeling inside had begun to manifest. Then, not only did I not have answers for my own direction, I began to feel defeated. Once I began to lose stuff I felt worthless. I had put my value in things. Then when the things were gone it impacted my thinking, because I did not understand how I could get people to buy into the idea that I was okay and still heading toward the greatness they were expecting. The pedestal that was established for me, how could I maintain it? I didn't have the answers.

I was a young girl overwhelmed with a child. I didn't know at that point if I was even able to parent. I sure didn't feel like it. I felt defeated. In all the emotions of defeat, I laid in bed in tears. Finally, I cried, finally, I released the anxiety and the feelings of defeat through tears. Finally, I let go of feeling responsible for finding answers to questions I was not capable of answering. I literally cried myself to sleep. I will never forget that moment, because it was pivotal in me finding myself. Like I said I cried myself to sleep that night. I remember it like it was scene from a movie, because when I retell or think of it, it sounds fake.

But, I was in bed, pillow soaking wet and I dozed off. In a four-bedroom house pitch black, and my son was tucked-away in his bedroom asleep. Suddenly, I was awakened by a loud deep voice calling out "NIA." I jumped-up on mommy protector, a girl from the south suburb of Dolton, IL by way of Englewood on the South-side of Chicago, who will take out anyone trying to mess with me and mine mode. So, I boldly walked to the stairs ready, weaponless by the way, and I did not say anything, because I'm no fool. I'm not just going to tell the intruder where I am. So, I go downstairs and no one is there. In my head, I am thinking this is it. It's either me or you and at this point I was willing to do just about anything, because I felt hopeless, purposeless and the only reason I was living was for Dj and had something happened to me, he'd be surrounded by family, so I had nothing to lose in my thinking.

But, no one was there. I went back to my room and got in my bed and laid there on my back staring at the ceiling. I heard the loud deep voice again, "NIA." I was like, who the hell is that??? So, I sat there, silent saying nothing. This time I was thinking you're going to have to just come to me, because I didn't know what was going on. So, I sat there and no one came. At this point, I began evaluating my sanity. I started checking my surroundings. I walked into my son's room to see if he was there. I gazed out the window just to make sure that my normal was my normal, because I knew someone had called my name, not once, but twice.

I finally calmed down, laid on my bed again and began to doze-off. Then suddenly, I began to recall being a little girl. My mother had come home one-day from being with one of my great-aunts. She handed me a sticker that said, "New Faith Baptist Church International." I placed it on the wall panel. I was probably about 12 years-old maybe a little older, but I can remember staring at it. My mother seemed so happy and had a light about her when she came back from that place. I will never forget it, not just a glowing light, but like a load was lifted too,as if her burdens were removed. I wondered when I stared at the sticker what that place was like. I wondered what church was like. I never really went as a child, but there was something about that sticker that came from that place.

Years went by, who knows what happened to the sticker, but, I laid in bed and thought about my brother telling me he had joined that church and I should visit. At this point, in my twenties, I was not desiring to experience church folks. There was a picture painted from various passings that killed my childlike curiosity from when I gazed at that sticker. I would tell him, no thank you, kind sir. Then, my niece was christened, so I was obligated to be present at the church I imagined that I would visit one-day. It was exactly as I imagined, crowded with everyone seeming to be searching for something. Everyone was wearing a smile and dressed nicely. However, life had taught me a great deal about facades at this point.

Anyway, I experienced it. I allowed myself to be free in the moment and I was present in that place. Just as every other person who just visits church the pastor spoke directly to me, so it seemed. I even shed a tear, me, the girl who had buried all of her emotions. I then walked away and said, it was cool -- nonchalantly, knowing inside that I was touched by some kind of presence. That night in bed I recalled all of this, and I felt compelled to go back to that church, joined and accept Jesus Christ as my personal Lord and Savior on Sunday, March 23, 2008.

Identifying My Role in the Emotional Trauma Through Relationships: Relationships Require Boundaries, and Abiding by Boundaries Show Respect

Reference: Matthew 15:13 for things that life sow that are not of Christ that must be uprooted.

Chapter One

For years, people have said that I should write a book. I said over and over again that it was not my time as a response to their suggestion. I was processing life. I did not have answers, and I felt like I had an incomplete story. I had no idea of what I would write about or who I would write for or to. Then, I started to hear a lot on the topic of self-love. In the 90s, I never heard people talk about self-love. The more I heard about it, the more I wanted to evaluate my own experiences to see if I had been exercising self-love in my own life. So, I began reading through my journals, and that's when I realized I had my topic and that I could target people just like me, trying to figure it out through life's chaos. I realized then, too, that self-love is a journey in life that we arrive at daily.

My story does not start here, but surely this example began a self-examination; I was in my mid to late twenties when I went through a very emotional breakup. Not emotional because the person I was engaged to did anything wrong, but emotional because I had so much disappointment before that relationship. I had to do some soul searching. I had to evaluate why I allowed that relationship to go as far as being engaged when I knew it was incompatible with marriage.

The turning point for me realizing that I was on the wrong path was a long conversation with my father, who I did not grow up with as an influential part of my life. Well, not influential in a healthy way. I was, however, influenced by his absence. He explained to me who he was as a person when I was growing up and his issues, and why it was in some ways good that he was not around. I realized from that conversation that I was operating with a level of numbness when it came to relationships; I was just going through the motions. After all, I had no real hope that the men I was with could live up to the expectations that I truly desired in a man. My father never fulfilled the expectations that a father should live up to. I will talk about this more later, but I left a lot of space for men to fail me in relationships and opened the door for them to go.

Before that conversation, I was at a church service on a Thursday night. A Prophetess delivered the sermon as part of a women's conference. She said, "Don't get what you want and lose everything you had." As I was driving home after the service, I began to evaluate my progress or lack of progress. What I realized was that I had given so much of myself to build this idea of a relationship that I lost everything that had become so important to me. That's the typical story of many women. I know many of us fall into that trap for various reasons that have been tagged to parental issues, but I disagree. I think this society we live in has done its job on us. We have so much work to do to rebuild the confidence and foundation for healthy unions. Beyond coming from broken homes, we need a complete cultural shift. But that statement from the prophet was profound for me; it connected directly to the doubts about my relationship.

At this point in that relationship, I felt I had to speak up about how I felt. Mainly, because I wanted to dream again. In the process of trying to build something that was not brought together by God for marriage, I lost my dreams because I began to settle. It became, well, since we cannot do this, let's JUST do something else, or if you cannot do it, then I will JUST do it. If you do not have a purpose, I will help you seek it; we can find one together since you lack vision. All this became a heavy load as if I picked up a 300-pound rock and felt responsible for moving it from one destination to another.

In my head, I figured I was in my late twenties, and I was ready to have more children and begin a ministry of marriage. Having a family was something I always wanted. Then someone came along and said they wanted me to be their wife. It was as if God answered my prayers, and that was enough for me. I did not consult God before I began building expectations for this relationship, which turned out to work for me rather than against me because I learned so much about myself through the dysfunction. Like how I see love and marriage as simple things. I never weighed the complexities. In my naivety, I thought the foundation of marriage was the desire to want it. I thought men did what they had to do to make it come together. I thought the most challenging part was finding someone you would like to spend the rest of your life with. I also thought that when a love interest comes in as a friend, that made it easier.

I was wrong. There are so many things we have to factor into choosing. I'm not a bad judge of character. I typically attract people who presumably have good character. I told myself that all I wanted was someone who I could love. I figured as long as I could give love, the rest would work itself out. I did not have many romantic relationships, but when I decided that I was ready, I figured that was the foundation I would stand on. However, I had no example of this alone working.

So, what did I do? I went after someone who needed love. I did not weigh into that notion once I gave what would be my source to replenish? What would be the return on my investment? That may sound selfish, but look at it this way, when Jesus hung on the Cross, there was a return for His sacrifice, and that is access to God. He gave us repentance regardless of our sin so that there would be a larger army to fulfill God's mission here on earth. I did not consider the return or the mission. Even in my doubt, I still believed in the power of two people coming together in marriage; the power of those two people doubles, and so does the work. I began to realize, if you do not have that power, you do not have a marriage. I could not see myself getting replenished to do God's work in that relationship.

I wanted so badly to be a wife, and I had goals and plans and a vision for my life, but that could not manifest if I was invested in someone who did not have a plan or vision for their future. I soon learned that I was being depleted. So I ran to the church to be filled, and the only thing I would find were reasons why I should let go.

I remember going to pre-marital classes at my church. I am a very observant person. I read body language, and the unspoken things within comments made very well, meaning when people say one thing, but you know through how they're saying it that they want to say something else, but may feel uncomfortable sharing how they feel. So, there was this older couple in the class, and I respect the wisdom of my elders very much. The guy of the two seemed very concerned about my relationship in a silent way. When my fiancé, at the time, would speak, he would challenge the things that he would say and give looks of doubt and concern. He would also share stories about his daughters and how he would be concerned about them and their decisions, and all this made me wonder what he saw as a man. Surely, I want what I want, and I won't abandon a plan on account of someone else's opinion, but I began to question things myself. I had a conversation with my ex-fiancé about the guy and how he seemed to be attacking him. He mentioned he noticed but could not understand why. I learned from this that sometimes you have to pay attention to silent advice. Question, the abrupt, loud advice, but it's something about the advice that comes subtly that houses the truth.

I needed that. One reason I can appreciate a church family is because your own family may be broken in areas. Although, my father helped me understand myself. This guy showed me how a man, a father cares about a daughter, not that I was his daughter in his eyes, but he could identify a problem as he would've with his daughters. I'm sure he would have been more vocal with his daughters; I understood that his heart had been shaped to have compassion for young women like me, who are trying to figure it out without a lot of information but desire to do the right thing.

Relationships are tough. Seeing that we are imperfect people, we all come into situations with issues; as my friend would say, "It's just a matter of what you're willing to deal with." I think that is very true, so I had to evaluate what I had dealt with. Between the ages of 15-30, I had three relationships. One was on and off for seven years. That was my son's father. I'm chalking that one up as being young; I was 15 years old. What was I thinking? I was not thinking; I was simply doing. I had to think about what role I played in that relationship. The other was short spanned after my son's father; I think I did more harm in that relationship than any other because of the timing. Hurt people, hurt people. Then, it was my fiancé. I talked much already about that relationship, but it was the greatest teacher. The more interesting thing is I was grounded in Christ even more by this time, so I thought

I had it right. The more I prayed about the relationship, the more I felt instructed to love him unconditionally. To this very day, I don't know why God's only words throughout were "love him."

I wanted to curse, yell at times, punch him (I am dealing with me; don't judge), but I maintained my character and followed instructions. I knew we had ended, but I would still check in with him, offering him prayer and praying for him. I know that ending something you had your hopes up for could cause emotional trauma, even more, when you may see every situation in your life as failed. So, I had to do my part to end it as best I could and be obedient to what God was telling me to do. But, unfortunately, I did get myself in it and had I prayed first, it probably would not have gone as far as it did.

Why, though, why would I do this to myself? Why didn't I pray first? I did not understand. This drove me into worry, which led to a panic and feeling overwhelmed because my ego did not want to believe that I made a bad decision that I would have to walk away from and say I messed up. I messed-up, because here I was in a relationship with someone who faced abandonment and disappointment over and over again. I agreed that I would be there. I decided that I would love, and love is enduring. Since I knew that, in panic, I said to myself that I would not give up. I changed my mind and decided that I was going to keep my word. I believed that God's grace would lead me through it. So, once I found that peace, something changed. We got distant, and he began to shut down, which I understood. I knew it was already too late to recover after all my questions and concerns from my worrying. It just ended abruptly. Right after I decided in my heart that I did not care about what I would receive, I made a promise, and I was sticking to my word.

After the abrupt end with no explanation and no closure, I began to question my decision-making. I began to question who I was? If I had learned anything in Christ? If I had grown any? My purpose, because I believed that I was a wife. I feared I would shut down emotionally. I did not know how to face my family, my friends, or my church. I know I walked around with a smile while I felt I was dying inside because I was known to be wise and strong, but here I am, broken like the many women who come to me for advice. Then I got into my feelings. I denied my desire to be a wife. I suppressed that desire because I had been disappointed. I began to accept that maybe I was supposed to be single and commit myself to the missions I was called to. I was a single mom already, so I am experiencing the joys of being a mother because God had already allowed that. Since I had the training, I figured I could carry that on to the children in the world who lack parenting in some form.

I was settling, though. Although I went chasing the city living, wanting nice cars, higher education, business endeavors, and relationships, a part of my soul was not satisfied. All those things were great, but I realized I was chasing them to fill a void. The truth was, I wanted a family.

That experience taught me that I was not as ready to give as I thought I was. The truth is, in a partnership/relationship, you have to understand the cost of love. You have to know that it is God's doing and not your own because we can commit to something or someone that is not meant for our destiny, and we'll spend years in a fight we should not even be in. I am a person of my word; what I speak will always come back to remind me of what I committed to through speaking it, like when I said that I would keep my word. As I was struggling with letting that relationship go, an elder woman at my church, without knowing my struggle told me that I should read Proverbs 6:5,(NIRV) "As a deer frees itself from a hunter, free yourself. As a bird frees itself from a trapper, free yourself."

At that point, I knew it was time to let go in August 2012. I let that go to later enter into something similar almost exactly one year after. I had just started law school in the Fall of 2013. I was reviewing the syllabus for my first class when I got a text. The text was from my son's new barber from the neighborhood I grew up in. The text was straightforward, with him asking me out. But, before I said yes, I told him I would have a phone conversation with him, and we talked for hours that night. I should back-track for a moment; I knew he had a crush on me when I took my son to see him because he was very nervous and smiling constantly, but he couldn't look me in the face; it was flattering.

We had many friendly back-and-forth conversations on Facebook before the text. He told me on that phone call that he has some baggage because he had two kids from a previous relationship and that their mother was trying to get on her feet, explaining as they were getting older, they realized their lack of compatibility, but ultimately, he wanted to be with someone he could build with, and considering my last relationship, surely I could relate and wanted the same thing. I put him on hold with the idea of dating him for about two weeks and a few nights' prayers and decided to move forward and date him. I figured it would be a slow and steady experience considering his circumstances and that I had just started graduate school. And, in the beginning, it was slow and steady. We took time to enjoy one another. We were really like old friends that grew up together. Around April 2014, I believe it was when he saw things going further because he asked me my thoughts on just allowing his kids to move out of town, knowing their mom did not have an income, and I thought it was unnecessary. I had no issue with their mom, and he was progressing personally from my perspective, and I thought time would sort it all out. That should've been a red flag to me, but I convinced myself that he would work it out because, from what I saw, he really wanted our relationship. I did my best to assure him that I was interested in him and that I planned to be with him and end up in a long-term relationship with him, marriage. We discussed marriage, and he knew that was a requirement for me. I did not like the idea of living together unmarried nor being a "wifey" I told him that I am a wife by biblical definition, flawed but proverbial 31 nonetheless.

Things were going well, and then around mid-year 2015, a few issues popped up; not baby momma drama, like one, would assume (if it were any drama in that area, he did a great job keeping it out of our relationship), but character flaws. Serious neediness is what I noticed and this relentless desire not to be left alone. It just seemed like he carried a constant fear. To mask these insecurities, he would use jealousy tactics to affirm my position in his life. I indeed questioned if he was for me because of this. I explained to him what I observed and why I thought it was an issue, and he eventually let it mull over, and in time we were okay. Then, in late 2015 I got pregnant. The moment I found out I was pregnant, he was the first to know, and it was very early in my pregnancy. I was excited but had some concerns about our future because he never really addressed the neediness issue that I saw. When I probed him because I know myself, I am a worker. I love the work that I do, I am educated, and I had no plans to waste that, and my career and service are very important to me. A man I am with has to understand that, but he assured me that was fine with him, and he followed by saying, "Nia, you don't want to have my child." Of course, I did not want him to think that, so I let up. At this point, you may be able to see that my concern was his using our child as an attempt to control me because, in my eyes, he had this depth of insecurity in maybe feeling like he was not good enough just as he is. So, he needed something to make him worth keeping, but as I said, I let up.

At this point, pregnant, I was in law school, working a full-time job and mentoring in journalism; along with that, I sought ways to enhance my writing skills to become a screenwriter, so I took a trip to the Sundance Film Festival in Park City, Utah. I was building my life, preparing for a new baby and a financially solid future. We did not spend as much time together, but we would text and check-in to make sure we were doing the things we had planned to do. I made it my business to invest in his endeavors because I knew the insecurities he held, so I wanted him to know, even with my absence, that I was in full support of his dreams and goals like they were my own. Before my trip, though, he told me something that shocked me that his kids moved out of state. It saddened me, but we had to keep pushing forward. I said we would do what we have to do to make him a part of their lives as normal as if they were at home. Then suddenly, months later and a few months before I had my daughter, like February 2016, he said my kids are coming back. I said, okay, let's sit down and come up with a plan. When we did that, he avoided the conversation, and I told him that I was done with the relationship because of his inability to make life decisions with me. In my mind, a person has to be able to own and face their issues and be responsible enough to employ an adequate moral compass to make the right sacrifices for the things they want in life. When he overlooked my concern about his neediness, he decided we did not need to discuss it, which excluded me, and was not owning his hang-up.

Along with that, when he allowed his children to move, he did not at least ask my opinion to include me in such a life-altering decision. Had he, I would have explained that my thoughts were he would be opening the door to his fear of being alone because, in a way, I felt they were his crutch in not facing that fear because I would not move with him until we bought a home together. He had some personal issues that he had to sort out before a marriage. I did not think he was mentally prepared to face that fear. I never had an opportunity to express that ~ time has allowed my thoughts to become true. But, in a nutshell, it was over just like that. I am raising my daughter alone, and for me, that's okay.

I never got an explanation on their sudden departure then return, but I will say I had a gut feeling there were lies embedded in his lack of disclosure. Before him telling me the kids were coming back, he said, "I need you to take care of me." When I heard that, I heard a broken soul, and the depth of his wounds required something that I did not have to give. I had to put my destiny first. It was hard because the nurturer in me wanted to find out what he needed and why his soul was crying out the way it was, but I had already been through enough to know that I could not fix him.

Even with the grotesque abandonment of a child, I cannot be angry with a man who is stuck in boyhood at the point of his abandonment issues. There is no progress in dwelling in anger because my destiny will be fulfilled; with him, I realized that I have learned how to choose myself over the years with all the mistakes.

Furthermore, the child we have together has an emotionally and psychologically whole mother who can teach her that it's okay to be alone and that she doesn't have to live with the constant fear that she's not good enough just as she is. Although he abandoned her, he'll one day realize that he abandoned a part of himself because that's the part of him that he never healed. That is the part of him that he ignored when I held up the mirror and brought it to his attention. Like his, the abandoned part of me is a piece of me that I grew to know so well but overcame.

Even with that relationship, I desired to love, but I have evidence now that loving myself first is more important. I never lingered on if I had made the right decision. Instead, I gave what I had to give, and when that was not enough, I moved on.

Self-evaluation:

Please journal your answers on the empty pages provided at the end of the chapter.

What is self-love? It is defined by Merriam Webster as love of self, or regard for one's own happiness or advantage.

What is self-worth? It is defined by Merriam Webster as a feeling that you are a good person who deserves to be treated with respect. I wanted to provide the simplest definition of these words because these characteristics of humanity are not complex. After all, we come here as infants with them, but along the trials of life, we lose them, but to get back to them, I am proposing we ask ourselves three questions:

1. What are my non-negotiables?
2. What areas do I set boundaries, and who is required to abide by them?
3. What are my personal standards?

Of course, I would never propose questions that I am not willing to provide answers to myself, and I will share with you why these questions are significant to me.

What are my non-negotiables: I learned after a few bad relationships that I cannot handle a liar. A person who finds it okay to lie over small things has that trait ingrained in their character. I can forgive them, but I cannot partner with them. For me, in partnership, I need trust and transparency. A person willing to lie about small things is not ready for where God is taking me. Your character has to be intact; you cannot move on fear and insecurities. I learned many men lie because they fear the outcome of the truth. If I find you're lying, the outcome will be what you fear; I will drop you because I feel you're too heavy of a burden for my destiny. I need you to move light and to be authentic along the way. So I have decided that a liar is a non-negotiable for me. I stick with the old saying that if you lie, you cheat, and if you cheat, you steal. A liar robs you of the truth, which can, in turn, cheat you out of progressing.

What areas do I set boundaries and who is required to abide by them: My atmosphere of influence is very important. I will not hold an audience with people I have a gut feeling are coming with a hidden agenda. If you want to meet and talk with me, you have to give me why you would like to meet with me and what you would like to accomplish. I have learned when I request this from people, they change their minds about the meeting. See, manipulative people know if they can get you to oblige to something quick, they got you. That is much easier to do face-to-face than over the phone or in an email because most people have a problem with telling people no. Anyone outside of my immediate and close extended family is required to abide by this rule. This one can get tricky, though, because some people will try to be slick. I had an occurrence when someone called my phone late and left a message saying, call me back; I have some great news to tell you. It was around 9 pm, for me, that was late, considering that I never permitted this person to call me outside of business hours. I look at it like this, I am an open book. People know when I am in a relationship, and if it's serious, people know I have children, and people know that I work. Considering those three things, I would think that would be a signal to a person to send an email after a certain time. I need my time, whether with my kids, with a significant other, or simply alone; I need that. It shows me the level of respect you have for me if you do not even ask me if it is okay for you to call me for personal things outside of business hours. If you were excited at the moment and you thought of me, that is one thing, but if I address it and you are offended that I would even consider 9 pm late, you do not respect my boundaries, and I am right in setting them. People want to see how far they can go and how serious you are about who and what is in your life.

What are my personal standards: I matter so much to myself that I will not let just anyone in my life. Clearly, by this chapter alone, you can see that I am not perfect. However, I apply equally yoked to the many areas of my life. I don't lie, I don't cheat, and I don't steal. I like to lead by these three things. If you accept doing one, you will probably do the others because doing one will produce the other if you really think about it, so I do not allow these three things free access into my life. I also do not like to be around people who willingly lie, cheat, or steal. You don't get a pass for me on these. If I find out and you do not clean it up right away, I am done. Deception wounds go deep, and it's hard to uproot betrayal. Although many people choose to fight through it in marriage, if it shows up before marriage, we should take it seriously and rethink if that person is ready for marriage.

Identifying My Experiences with Rejection/Abandonment

Reference: 1 Peter 2:4 As you come to him, the living Stone—rejected by humans but chosen by God and precious to him

—

Chapter Two

I can say that I always carried a sense of unconditional love for people regardless of who they were. It could've been just an innate innocence, but life experience can cause that to dissipate slowly. I remember being a kid doing just about anything for anyone. I was born with a servant's heart. I wanted everyone to be happy. I always felt like it was a gift. As I grew older, I learned that people could be manipulative and use good to their advantage. As a teenager, I began to allow that to change me. I became an introvert. I was still kind, friendly, and somewhat social, but I was very picky about who I let in. I would hang with everyone, but I would not consider them friends or let them in, and that taught me that people do not like that. People do not like when you don't let them in, and later in life, I learned that helps identify people with rejection issues. As a teenager, though, I could not identify it, and it probably caused me to rub people the wrong way. Especially girls, guys did not care because they somehow don't get the same jealous Spirit that we have to learn to relinquish. Guys often seemed used to the rejection or just did not care, but females were different. If you reject them, they become catty, spiteful, and hateful. I saw it in high school, college, work environments, and yes, even the church. That was hard for me to navigate through.

Not allowing people in typically had nothing to do with the other person. I just did not have the desire to nurture relationships. I had my core friends, and that was enough for me. I can think all the way back to being in elementary school and having girl cliques. There was a type of clique for every girl. I was from the city and moved to the suburbs in third grade. It took me a little time to make new friends, but I had to go from clique to clique until I found which one worked for me. Ultimately acquired one friend who I still talk to today. My good friend, Georgia, hit it off quickly. It's like we understood each other from the jump. We were trapped in a suburban world that took some getting used to. I think she admired my style, too, because she still makes fun of my choker necklace and bodysuits with baggy jeans. Style was important to me because I went through a lot to steal clothes from my cousin Saundra and match them with things from my mother's jewelry box.

I still take my mother's things. That little girl in many of us never grows up; whether it's the one who rejects others or was rejected, she traveled with most of us to adulthood. Childhood rejection creates problems in building relationships as adults, especially with women. We women need one another for many different reasons. We work together and go through some of the same issues, where we could stand one another's support. But, unfortunately, our warped mentality will sometimes influence us to put up a guard that hinders us from getting to know each other and how we could benefit from one another, or we fight and tear one another down.

This issue comes from somewhere for each of us. We build walls, sabotage, cling, or become co-dependent, but whatever we use to cope, it's all rooted in something from our childhood.

I will never forget when I was around seven years old. My mom, brother, and I lived in the south suburbs of Chicago; as I mentioned, I moved from the city while in elementary school. However, we still had extended family that lived in the heart of Englewood, a high-crime area of Chicago. The block my family lived on; every house was occupied by a piece of history for me. My mother would drop me off at my grandfather's house on weekdays very early in the mornings in the summer. I would sit on the porch and wait for the elders to take a seat on their porches, and I would sit and just listen to their wisdom.

One day, I sat on the porch, and I gazed up and saw a man standing on the rooftop across the street. The house belonged to my father's family. When I looked up, surprisingly, I saw a man who resembled my estranged father. As I squinted my eyes to make clear who I thought I saw, the man waved at me. At that point, I knew it was him because what father would not recognize his daughter? I am the type of person who must do something when I get excited because I don't like to be overwhelmed by any emotion. So I jumped up and went to make myself a cold drink and grabbed a snack, and I went back to the porch. When I sat down, I noticed the truck was pulling off. In my head, I was creating this moment that my dad would come and hug me and tell me how much he missed me. That was the very first time in my life I felt abandoned and rejected. I thought my father had a legit reason for not coming around, but that moment made me feel somewhat unlovable. After that, I went on with my life. I had my mother and my brother. As I grew older, my peers liked boys, but my heart hardened. I was not the young girl who desired a boyfriend. I honestly did not look at boys. I was 15 years old when I thought about liking boys back. I'm sure that worked for my mother and my brother. But those cutesy, puppy love moments that kids have, I did not have. I was emotionless. I am not sure if that is where emotions are developed; I missed it.

I shared the story about thinking I saw my father because, for years, I harbored feelings of always being rejected because of something I created in my head. I don't even know if that was my father or an uncle or cousin who just knew of the family across the street. I held on to these negative feelings from childhood. In every relationship that I entered, I expected the guy to leave. I figured if my own father would not want to stay, why would a boy that had no obligations. When I was 15 years old, there was this boy that I knew of before high school, but like the others, I paid him no attention. He pursued me relentlessly. He may not like that description, but everyone he knew and knew me reminded me that he had a thing for me. I ignored them, and he graduated and went away for military training. I thought we would not see each other again. I did not want to address the fact that I was afraid to talk to boys, but then school started back, and at this point, I was a sophomore, and he came back. Because of my feelings about my father, I initially did not take his persistence and his pursuit seriously.

I had to own that I was doing that to myself. I created that hurt, not my father. Of course, not being in my life was a gateway to that idea, but he did not place that experience there. Every failed relationship was an opportunity for me to see that it was me. I learned that I always assumed men would leave because I held on to this fear of rejection. I would always set up an exit strategy for men. I did not want to believe they even desired to stay around because I did not see that as a trait that men were capable of.

This mindset did not just stem from my father, I believe that is where it started, but I was very close to my grandfather. He died when I was seven years old. He was my father when my father was not around. He died abruptly.

I remember sitting on the porch as he walked to his big brownish-tan car to go to a doctor's visit, and I yelled out, "granddad, will you bring me back some overalls like yours." He said, "yes, what color, blue or black." "Blue," I said.

I waited and waited because he always kept his word with me, so I was expecting him and my overalls. As little girls, we admire the men who care for us, and he did just that all the time. He would always make sure when I came over that he had my favorite cinnamon rolls on the kitchen table or my fifty-one cents to get my cheese doo doos and grape quarter juice from the corner store, never failed. So the day he left to go to the doctor, I wasn't worried about him coming back because he always did.

Then, suddenly, my entire family was frantic. I remember my mother telling me that my grandfather had died. I did not believe her at first. I was still expecting him to come home. My aunt, who went to identify him, came home in tears, explaining to us that he had an aneurysm on the train and was found dead. I think I went in some type of shock because my nose started to bleed in true young Nia fashion. Any trauma, drama, or discomfort would cause my nose to bleed when I was a kid, I think I was born with too much blood, and that's how my body purged of it. (laughing)

I am pretty sure that was the moment I had settled in my heart that people you love leave, so it is pointless to get attached. That's when I learned the self-abusive trait of moving on without really grieving or taking in the reality of a loved one's death. So I just sucked it up and moved on with life.

I sit in Panera Bread, recalling this crying like a baby

among all these strangers. I could not say if that experience was rooted in abandonment or rejection issues. Still, it definitely made me even more numb to emotions. I would say it opened up issues with rejection, too, because I don't like to set myself up for rejection through caring about people. I reject sharing friendships and relationships with people because my expectation of them staying around is very low.

If I let you in, I always say that you are very special because I open up to very few people, but I am a very transparent person. In some way, I feel my transparency is the gateway to showing people I care. I'm just not going to get comfortable -- I am not emotionally open to anyone, but since I have acknowledged this and where it started, I have grown gradually. I have learned that life is about seasons. I have accepted that people come and go. I have accepted that people we love we see again if they are saved. Let me tell y'all when I got that in my Spirit, I handed every family member the prayer of salvation with chocolate attached (laughs). We are ride or die on earth as well as in Heaven. My Jones click, my grandfather's lineage.

So, when I go back to my issue with women, I learned it's not all of them. Part of it is me and the hurt I harbored from my past. I had to find out what it was to me that people wanted or needed. I had to understand how God wanted to use me, so I acknowledged my weaknesses so that through Christ, I could be strengthened and begin to operate in my anointing without shutting people out because I was hurting.

It's always those moments for me when I would have deep conversations, sometimes very personal conversations with another woman. I have always been a sounding board for people. I am not mad at that. It's actually one of my favorite qualities about myself. But, still, because I do listen and hear a person in a moment in my thinking, I am not defining that as a friendship; this is where I am always confused because women will see it differently. They will call after the conversation hoping to hang out, and I will be thinking to myself that I cannot, I won't, and don't even desire to.

I am thinking to myself that it was a moment. We as women should be open to those moments as a form of solidarity and understanding that we all just want to be heard and acknowledged and share testimony to learn that whatever we are going through will be okay. Share the moment, cherish the moment, then get back to life, energized, replenished because you had an encounter with a sister. But, for years, I was wrong. Women would turn on me and be angry towards me. The anger projected at me forced me to address or evaluate my own issues. I tried to find the points of pain, and I evaluated my relationship with my parents first. I thought, well, since I am having issues with women, what is my relationship with my mom?

I was most afraid to travel down this path because a Black mother is sacred. Nothing touches a Black mother, not even your own pain you have to heal, culturally we bury momma hurt because that's momma. However, I realized that I am almost way too protective over my mom in my self-reflecting. My mom always had this confusing soft but extremely tough side, but it never fooled me. She would do or give to anyone, and being her youngest and daughter; I watched her every move. I heard her words, but more than that, I saw her actions. We never had an affectionate relationship, but in my twenties, I began to think maybe we shared that same numbness I chose when granddaddy died, but for her, she may have gone numb when her mother died, right before I was born.

I became a mother in my twenties; my mother was 23 years old when she had me. I could not imagine having to be a mother after losing mine. I needed my mom with each child. Every experience is so different, and on top of that, those little pieces of advice that she gives as I navigate through parenting are so valuable. People like to tell you if you grow up in a single-parent home, you should find other women to look up to if you want to marry because your mother cannot teach you that. I feel like it applies in some areas, but when it comes to Ilene's (my grandmother) girls, she instilled something in them that made them good solid, loving women. I think some women are just too good to be played with, and my mother is one of them. I had to challenge my feelings about her, though, because I needed to know if there was any resentment there or feelings of abandonment because she had to do everything, but I realized there wasn't, and we had an aunt who was a gap filler, my aunt gave all the hugs and encouraging words and having that helped.

So, in gaining that self-awareness, I learned, with women, I had my experiences as a young adult, but as a maturing adult, what I have learned over the years is that women who harbor the issues of rejection and abandonment display bad behaviors, for example, jealousy and envy.

As adult women, what happens is that we have this foothold, if you will, or feelings of abandonment or feelings of rejection, and it shows up sometimes through jealousy. So, let me break down my understanding of this, so what happens is we have these feelings right, and they're negative feelings. We have a negative feeling that stems from something that happened to us that we never addressed. So, we see other women thriving, and we see other women being successful, and we see other women working through their issues progressing through life still having issues, but they work through them. They're not stuck; they don't seem to be caught up in the wrong things with the wrong people that hinder their lives, and to people on the outside, they are living the life they desire to live. So, we don't see perfection in these women, but they are operating through life even with issues and still finding joy in their day-to-day lives with traumatic experiences.

I had to think, maybe this is what others who wanted to connect with me saw, because I was not perfect and because I had my mistakes and was transparent about them, but I was definitely one who pursued what I wanted in life. So I thought maybe that desire to connect, they possibly want to know with my issues how do I keep going and that's why I said before in this chapter that I had to learn how God was using me.

Because ultimately, none of us are different to a degree; we all have drama, trauma, mess, and stuff that we must sit through and figure out. So, when you have these issues and feelings of abandonment and of rejection, and we never address it to get to a place of understanding, we can put up walls and unnecessary hurdles, as I did. Or, for some of us, the reoccurring experience of rejection just hinders us, and that's why uprooting these negative emotions is essential because they are a seed that you can water with experiences and encounters. What those seeds will produce much of the time in women are jealousy and envy. The more you feed it, the more it grows, the more it grows, the heavier we become, and we will spend our life looking at other people and analyzing other people, being critical of other people, holding commentary about other people, and not fertilizing our own life with good. The more you pay attention to what other people have going on and do not evaluate our own issues; we're feeding that place of abandonment and rejection, and it shows up as jealousy and envy, and we cannot help but see others in a jealous light when we do this. We get to a place where we become professional commentators and spectators over other people's lives while our is in shambles from things we never seek to address.

Because we are relational, we gravitate to what we like and what we see and who we want to connect with, and traits in other people that we want to connect with. It is inevitable, so the people that we watch and see-through negative lenses, in true reality, we admire them. But we women never acknowledge it that way, maybe because that first encounter did not go the way we desired, then that person becomes the target of our negativity. In reality, we want to connect because we see ourselves in them; everything in us is looking at them as a model of what we want to do or who we want to be. But, because we have this seed that we fertilized with negativity, we cannot grow or become what they have learned by doing their work.

As a woman, I have learned our own feelings of rejection and abandonment are not unique to just some particular women or those who grew up in a fatherless home or those who may have issues with their mother.

It is something that we all experience, so we should stop this torment that we do to each other in calling out daddy issues or mommy issues; we all have daddy and mommy issues to a degree whether you grew up in the household with him or whether your father left. Or whether your mother was present or not. We have to stop calling people out for not having something because we did and making them feel bad about it when each of us is dealing with something, spoken or unspoken.

In the Black community, if someone grew up without a father, it is very sick in my eyes for black men to hold that against a woman and say all she got daddy issues or she can't keep a man because she has daddy issues, or for women saying that he can't keep a woman because he has mommy issues that is not what a community does to one another. We embrace people whether they grew up without or if they grew up with, and we don't hold it against them. If they do have issues because of that, we can give them a space to talk about it, but to hold it against them and make them feel less than because of it; that's one thing in the black community that we have to stop. So, as I said, these feelings of rejection and abandonment are not subjective to a certain type of upbringing; we all have dealt with these issues regardless of our upbringing. We all have them, but we have to learn how to navigate through them and not allow them to overcome us or develop into bad behaviors where we're hurting people because we're hurt.

As I said before, I went on my tangent, we as women, as we are maturing, must know that many of us have these issues of rejection and abandonment. We must learn how to feed that with positivity; that's why when we see other sisters, other women, we should acknowledge them, hear them, and make them feel seen. Regardless of how we feel, it should be common practice because it feeds positivity and affirms us and maybe the other woman. I am happy when I can make another woman smile or feel good about herself because I know how hard we are on ourselves. I also know what kind of internal stuff we battle. Women, we have our issues with each other, and it doesn't matter how much we evolve; we probably will never get rid of the issues we have among each other, but there's no need to be nasty toward one another. I am glad I have been able to reconcile my confusion because I can move through life better, having better relationships with women. And knowing why I have chosen the relationship I have in the past.

Self-evaluation:

Please journal your answers on the empty pages provided at the end of the chapter.

1. What painful experience am I suppressing?
2. How do I address it?
3. What do I learn about myself after I address it?

What painful experience am I suppressing: For me, it was when I assumed I saw my father. I had to narrow down what issue continued to show up in my life, and it was my relationships with men. What shapes how we see relationships is through our parents; even more than that, as women, we see men typically through our fathers. When I narrowed that down, I had to say in my entire life, I never hated my father for not being there, but why did I recall this moment? I also had to evaluate my feelings at the moment and what feelings they brought up when I thought about it. As I said, I felt abandoned at that moment, but I also felt a numbness come over me like I just turned something off, like hope. Imagine living life and entering relationships with no hope. On top of losing my grandfather abruptly, as I explained, that created complete hopelessness in this area.

I learned that hopelessness is rooted in depression, but it can also be triggered by negative life events. I always say that emotions are internal GPS leading you to the root of a problem. So instead of ignoring them, we should pay close attention to them. Although I could not identify the feeling at the time, what I felt was hopelessness, I realized it kept showing up in every relationship. Because I would just give up. In each connection, I had no hope for future success, and viewing them going any further would lead to negativity in my eyes.

Now, I do not regret any of the relationships ending, but I had to ask myself if I choose men that I know wouldn't work, knowing it would end eventually.

How do I address it: I addressed that particular pain by accepting the truth. I did not know I created this narrative in my thinking that shaped me, and I just did not know if that was the truth. So first, I had to stop the story. Then I had to ask myself what void I needed to fill to stop telling myself that story because even though the idea was painful, thinking about it over and over again filled something.

It was simply the absence of my parent. So, I had to think, I can't fill that. By the time I realized this, I was in my twenties, and I could not go back. So, I had to begin to think about what was true. What could I replace that narrative with? My truth was that I had a grandfather that loved me unconditionally and showed it. I knew through him what it felt like to be loved, protected, and cared for. Not only that, I had my uncles who stood in gaps after my grandfather died and those that my father did not fill – my village was strong.

At the point of realization, my father had come back into my life, so I had to factor that in and just work on our relationship and be open to having one with him that would help me navigate through relationships.

What did I learn about myself after I addressed it: I learned it was a self-sabotaging pattern. I would assume something, come to a conclusion, then live a lie based on a narrative I put in my head based on a fear of rejection and abandonment. Although the fear of rejection show-up in all types of relationships, abandonment was the one I feared the most, so I shaped my thinking to just cut people off before they could cut me off.

I do believe since we are human innately that we are relational. So, it's normal to want to be connected to people. But, suppose you find yourself isolating or easily abandoning people. In that case, you need to dig to see what's up with you because it's not normal. But, I did not feel like it was not normal; I felt okay with relationships just ending and moving on abruptly.

I also learned that I could move forward without guilt, regret, or shame even with all that happened. I learned that I still could build some good solid relationships, so I was capable; I just had not manifested what I desired in marriage. With women, I learned that I can be clear about my intentions and upfront about my views on friendships and that I am a bit of an introvert. If a friendship happens, I began to accept that it would happen organically. I just could not burden myself with what other people walk away with as long as I knew my intentions were upright. I don't seek "tea," and I am not spreading no one's business, so I know for me, even if it's their fear, it's not who I am.

Learning to Forgive - It was a Process

Reference: John 14:26 But the Helper, the Holy Spirit, whom the Father will send in my name, he will teach you all things and bring to your remembrance all that I have said to you.

Chapter Three

When you go through something in life, a hard thing to do is to forgive yourself when it does not turn out the way you expected; we must get to the place where you forgive you and take it to God and pray. Regardless of what it is, if it is a sin, repent and let go of the guilt; it is already done in God's eyes. He wants us to turn away from it because he does not want us constantly going through the same thing over and over again. After all, it keeps us from fulfilling the purpose He created us for. It distracts us.

I remember the feelings of guilt when I left my job to pursue my dream of being an entrepreneur. As you know by now, I am a single mother. Not only was I afraid that I would not meet my son's needs, I went through spiritual freight, questioning who God created me to be in my ability to create wealth. Those fears created doubt, and the doubt produced more fear, which had me desperately seeking alternatives to make money instead of focusing on building my business. My fears interfered with my faith. To move forward, I had to forgive myself for feeling guilty about taking a chance. What brought me to the decision to leap, wait, as you all may remember from the introduction, I had a bit of an ego. We all know change is a process that does not happen overnight. By this time in my spiritual life, I had been saved for about 3-years, and I was learning to discern God's voice over the doubts, fears, and areas of insecurities. I worked in risk management as staff support at a medical association, and I liked my job. I was comfortable with my pay; although I wanted more, it paid the bills. I was taking care of my son and was able to invest in starting an online magazine that I had desired since college.

Things were going well with me doing both. Until I launched it and went public with it. It seemed as soon as I let that thing loose, it took on a life of its own. It did not blow up with readership, but I began to see the possibilities. I saw it becoming ministry work. I began to see how God uses the gift of writing. My vision for it got larger; the more I dreamed, the more plans I wanted to make. Yet, I was being realistic with myself. This was not lucrative for me, so I continued to view it as something I would do aside from work. I then applied for a job at the company I was working for, a medical journal, because ultimately, I wanted to be in editorial production. I had the interview and was told that I was in a support staff position and there was no way that I could move up to become an editor. The company just did not work that way. I was disappointed, but I did some research on the organization's culture, and it was true. The likelihood of me moving up was hopeless. I was down about that because surely, I had no desire to stay in the position I was in; I liked the work I did, but it was not fulfilling, and I had student loans, I wanted to securely purchase a home and invest in my own published works, and that current position didn't fit the income bracket for the life I desired to live.

So, in October of 2010, I decided to give my employer the notice that I was going to depart from my position. I can remember when I left work that day, my last day of working in the fall of October, I just felt so liberated I felt so free, but I looked up at all the skyscrapers in Chicago as I was walking down Michigan Avenue and I thought to myself what the hell have I done. I had no clue of what I would journey through at that moment, but I knew that I was embarking on unknown territory for myself. The idea of having to find the income on my own to make sure that not only do I run a business, but I also provide for my son was scary. I took a deep breath, and I kept walking, and I smiled, and I just had faith at that moment that everything was going to be okay.

So, I had gotten me a small office in Homewood, Illinois, which is a south suburb outside of Chicago, and it was a little room in the basement, probably 200 to 300 square feet if that I can't remember, but it was small but in those four walls was a place that I could go and do my work. So, I immediately began to draft sponsorship requests trying to seek money from various resources and find ways to generate money. On top of that, I knew that I would have to get a part-time job just to pay my bills, to hold me afloat, but I wanted to do something mindless so that I would be able to build my company.

I was a little frantic as I was sending out sponsorship requests and looking for part-time work; I was all over the place where I could not figure out which direction I wanted to go. I had this vision for the magazine and the publishing company in the works that I wanted to do; I had that all lined up. I had my business plan. I had all the articles that I wanted to write. I had the website built; I went to Atlanta and had someone build a website for me early in February 2010, before I quit the job, so everything that I needed was in place. So, as I said, I had the space, I had the website, I had the vision for the magazine, but then I had to figure out how to make money to keep my life afloat, and that's what was my stumbling block. That was the thing that caused me to fail. I did not plan my finances well; I did not plan out how my company would be financed. I didn't pitch it to anyone. I did not look for any investors. I did not set up any revenue streams back then in 2010 the revenue streams for social media were not like it is today in 2021. We did not have access to monetize on social media platforms. We were able to use social media to market, but we were not able to monetize on social media platforms. I did have my website set up so that I could get ad revenue, I also put out information to place ads in my magazine, but that fell short because my target audience is everyday people, and so when you don't have the big corporations coming in to place ads and then you don't have the money 'cause you can't depend on the community that you want to reach to give you that big lump sum of money that you need to stay afloat, hire people and to produce the content that you need to be a real business. It became a whirlwind of confusion on how to make money, and the only way I knew how to make money was to be a worker, not an owner. I went through trying to host events and raise money through event hosting, all the things that are kind of normal when it comes to fundraising, so I did those things unsuccessfully. I did not have success, and I did not have a lot of turnouts.

Also, I wasn't growing an audience like I thought I would. And I thought I would grow an audience because initially when I started the magazine, it got a lot of feedback in a lot of positivity. People were speaking as if it was needed in our community, so one of the biggest things in business is to meet a need. When you're in business, that is one primary focus of what you do, and the question you ask yourself is, is there a need for this? So, when I launched it, it was all passion work, but when I launched it and saw that there was a desire for this to exist, that is what made me want to go full fledge in doing it. But when I got out there and started doing it, all that support dismantled, it was gone, I didn't have it. I would put stuff out there; no one would share it. I would write articles I would get no feedback. I would request to do interviews with everyday people, and people would not respond to it. But as a business owner, you never blame the people; you always think it's something that you can do better, something that you can do differently. So, I was trying different avenues, and I didn't want to be in spaces that I wasn't comfortable in. I was never very comfortable with entertainment news. I didn't have a desire to do fashion, didn't want to do gossip news. I wanted my niche to be what my niche is, so I just figured that I needed to do some more work for myself to create a better delivery.

I didn't want to fall into the category of the bitter business owner where I was blaming the people that I needed to build my company. I didn't want to blame them, and they are resources for content, everyday people; I focus on the greatness of everyday people, so that was very important for me to not seem as though I was angry at the readers, or the followers or the supporters because my vision wasn't coming to fruition the way that I wanted it to. So, I decided on my own that I needed to take a step back because I knew what I wanted to do, I knew that I wanted to do this magazine, and I know that I wanted to have a platform, a visual platform on YouTube, I knew that a media company that publishes works copyrighted works was a business that I wanted to own. So, I had to take a step back, and even with a step back, I was beating myself up because I felt as though I failed, I didn't feel as though I failed in my vision; I felt as though I failed in my delivery because I did not plan out how I wanted to execute this thing and maintain it financially. So, I had to do a deep dive into my understanding of business. Then I just got wrapped up in reading books on finances and books on copyright ownership and reading books on intellectual property and understanding what intellectual properties are and how I could come to carve out a career path in that.

My passion, of course, is what it is, storytelling that's what I love, but to make stories revenue gaining works, I had to understand intellectual property, so that's when I came across a program at John Marshall law school, now the University of Illinois at Chicago law school, where they had a master's degree that focused specifically on intellectual properties for non-attorney business professionals I felt as though God dropped that right in my lap. It was a program in law school keeping in mind that as a kid, I wanted to go to law school and become a lawyer, but as I grew up, I just didn't like a lot of the things that went into becoming an attorney and not the law aspect of it I always loved that, but just how it works. I just didn't like the dynamic of being an attorney and what you are up against to be one with morals. Still, I was able to do two things at once, fulfill a childhood dream by going to law school and understand how to build revenue with my intellectual properties in a master's degree program, so getting that degree, I actually did three things in one, because I knew that if I ever had to get back into the workforce having the master's degree would give me some leverage to at least get a job that paid well so that I can use it to leverage my business and gain some knowledge and build my confidence back up because at this point my confidence was broken because I just felt like a failure because I tried something that I loved but it didn't come to fruition; it didn't happen, so at this point, I needed to regain my confidence. However, I still hadn't realized at this point in desiring to regain my confidence that I had to factor in forgiving myself. Not forgiving myself for doing any of it but just forgiving myself by not being so hard on myself for failing forward. I failed forward I found something that could help me as a person that could help me intellectually that can help my business, so I failed forward, and I had to realize that, but to even realize that, I had to say, okay Nia, you're being too hard on yourself lighten up kid and take it for what it is.

I did that I began rebuilding my confidence. That's when I started writing more and talking about it. I decided to put myself in spaces with other creatives and owners to figure out how financing projects work. I also began to think back on my previous employer that I left and analyze their business structure and brainstorm how I can incorporate things into my business that I learned there in seeking funds and having a nonprofit extension of your business to raise money for projects to support the community. If I did not forgive myself, I would have never looked back at the company and found the good in the experience. The crazy thing is that I worked in the department and put together the agendas for oversight on funding going in and out of the organization. God put me in that space to learn. Just to go back a bit on how I got the job, I applied; I knew the HR recruiters because I held a contract position there in records keeping while I was in college. I left to go back into banking, I spent about 8 years in banking, but I went back there to branch into regional marketing, but the housing collapse happened in 2008, and it impacted banking heavily, people were being laid off, so I reached out, and I quit the bank, three months later I was hired back into the association with a permanent job. My son's grandmother worked there and had mentioned she talked to a director about a friend, and I was like, little did she know that the director saw my resume and assumed I was the friend. So, I kind of got the job by a fluke, but it was divine order. It was not an easy role. I did not like the director's managing style, but I learned so much from her in how believing in your abilities, hard work, and confidence get you respect. After I walked in the forgiveness, I was able to see that, also, how I was in the position to learn what I needed to know to do what God had for me to do.

Finally, forgiving my father – my work, not his.

Self-forgiveness, which I had to do for my work-life, was important, but also forgiving my father; forgiveness in those two areas were turning points for me because I knew my purpose was larger than merely existing. Leaving my job was bold; it helped me realize my purpose more; acknowledging my father giving me my name allowed me to see how God works, too - with the unforgiveness it blocked me from seeing God's greatness and His greatness in me.

Throughout the book, I mentioned a few times how my father played significant roles in my life, even in his absence. With one of those things being my name and where my name came from, my father decided that for me, and good thing my mother was respectful enough to allow him to make that decision. The biggest turning point for me was knowing that my father had given me something that meant so much to me. That made me want to evaluate how I felt toward him, which is not easy to do when you build this wall in your heart because you don't want to feel the emotions that go along with it. I had all these loving, caring relationships with other men; I continuously told myself that I did not need to welcome my father into my life because why would I want someone in my life who did not want to be in my life. But that was a part of the false narrative that I spent telling myself from childhood even until young adulthood that he did not want to be in life; he did. My mother nor family told me he did not; his absence made that argument itself and did a very good job making it.

In my heart, I had to forgive him. For the initial offense

of abandonment, I had to forgive him to walk in my true purpose, my divine purpose, because without forgiving him, I would be harboring baggage that was just too heavy of a load for me to carry. Being where I want to be in my career, where I want to be in my purpose and also in being a mother, a good mother to my children, if I carried that bitterness in my heart, it would have had to play out somewhere in my life, and, I would be damned if I would let that hold me hostage and impact my children or the relationship that I have with my kids, because of something that started from when I was a kid, I just couldn't bear that weight. I couldn't carry that load, and I could not put that onto my kids because my kids will have their own things that they have to figure out through life, and I want to help them navigate through those things without the baggage that comes from my childhood. So, I had to clean that up.

Finding my purpose was a turning point, but forgiving him to raise my kids was also a significant reason I thought it would be necessary. Now, I say that finding my purpose was a turning point in giving me my name because my name means purpose and finding out what my name meant was so substantial in me wanting to be exactly who I am. It really helped define me because it pushed me to seek heritage even deeper; it pushed me to seek my divine purpose, even more, it guided me to want to figure out why I'm here, because when I look into the principles of Kwanzaa, and I look into the principle, Nia, and to look back on generations and to carry on the legacies and things like that, to teach current generations about our history -- It made me want to begin to learn about all of that. It made so much sense to me and connected me to so many parts of me that pertained to where I was and what I wanted to do in life in writing. I got to a place of how the heck can I hold a grudge against someone who has given me so much in naming me?

That's why forgiveness is important; it is said that you do it for yourself, and you truly do it for yourself. You create a space in your heart when you forgive someone to be filled by God so that you can give more to the world. When you are what I called spiritually and emotionally congested, it's hard for that space to be filled for you to give what you need to give to this world because, ultimately, we are vessels. When we decide to give our lives to Christ or to take the faith walk through life, we have to be open to being usable vessels right when we crowd those vessels with emotional stuff, things that we can't let go of, things that keep us begrudging, things that keep us angry, ***things that keep us angry*** and I want to make a special note on things that keep us angry because anger is always the response to something much deeper when we harbor those things, whether it's rejection, abandonment, neglect, or abuse, regardless of what it is when we harbor those things, we do not leave an open space for God to pour his will into us or his desires for us. So, how can we give out to the world? That's why a lot of times we're giving out anger or giving out negativity, all the things that make this world such a corrupt and evil place.

I had to learn that I did not want to contribute to the negativity, so I wanted to relinquish and let go of all that stuff so that God could fill me with His stuff. And you know when you get to that place and have that open space, you start looking to fill it with positivity and good things. That's when I think that affirming yourself is important. That's when I think positive talking and positive affirmations are effective. And that's when I think that is the time to start putting the word of God into your heart because putting the word of God into your heart will give those positive affirmations in those positive things a foundation. If you are feeding yourself affirmations and positive talk and the foundation of your heart is negativity; the negativity and those damaging emotions are going to destroy positive talk and affirmations. It's only when you clear that stuff from your heart that you get to rebuild the foundation with something that is going to uphold you, and I believe that the word of God, especially psalms from the scriptures from the Book of Psalm. I think a heart built on scriptures from Psalm can really give you a good solid foundation to begin to affirm yourself with positive things with a positive mindset and a positive take on life works. It's heart work. It takes time. It takes building, but anything that is built to last must have a firm foundation. If you have been lucky enough for that foundation to begin in your childhood, that is amazing. Kudos to anybody who has had that life. But a lot of times, we must come into these realizations as we get older and fix a lot of things that went wrong in our childhood so that we can be effective, honest, transparent, authentic adults. Then, we can begin to pass that down as a legacy as well. Generational legacy building is not just about things; it's about being a good person too. Being an authentic person and loving in everything makes this world a good place; we must pass those things down and have good morals.

Yeah, so those things are important. And when I walked down the path of forgiving my father, that's when I began to open up to all of these things about what I wanted to pass down generationally. Trauma, hurt, heartbreak was not something that I desired to pass down. With an understanding that my children will go through their own experiences, and those things may come up. But without harboring them in having them as their ways of understanding. They will be able to walk through these emotions and gain an even better understanding if they are not victims of my claimed victimhood. That's important in raising kids.

Self-evaluation:

Please journal your answers on the empty pages provided at the end of the chapter.

1. Self-forgiveness allows you to separate from the mistakes you made.
2. Are you secretly begrudging toward a parent?

Self-forgiveness allows you to separate from the mistakes you made.

In recounting my experiences in this chapter, I realized how important it is to forgive myself for the mistakes that I made, especially in my relationships with family and decision-making. This is huge because when you can forgive yourself for your mistakes, it really opens the door for you to move forward in life. And I learned that I had to forgive myself for my mistakes, and mistakes are inevitable. We cannot go through life without making mistakes. We cannot grow without making mistakes. And that is the self-evaluation that I had to apply in forgiving myself. What have I done? What do I need to forgive? And how do I move on from there?

Are you secretly begrudging toward a parent: I already wrote about this a lot in chapter two, but that was more about the issues that came from a broken relationship with a parent. This, as you read, is about coming into a space of forgiveness with that parent. Chapter two breaks down how you really have to realize the issue, but after you do that, you have to forgive. We are always going to have memories and thoughts that remind us of how someone may have made us feel, but forgiveness, as I mentioned, is more for us than it is for them because it clears out our hearts, and we don't want to hold that grudge against them. Forgiveness frees us to be more of who we desire to be. So remember with your parents to check the little things, like the broken promise or the time when they lied, and we knew - get clarity on their reasoning. Ask them questions for closure if you can. If you cannot, go back to that moment and really ponder and pray over it. I know people don't like digging things up, but how you responded to that moment matters because you could be living in a narrative that is a lie. The truth sets us free.

Is it Better to be Single?

Reference: 1 Corinthians 7:8 -- Now to the unmarried and the widows I say: It is good for them to stay unmarried, as I do.

Chapter Four

Singleness is synonymous with mission for me. I have always been in this personal struggle where I want marriage for a family because I desire to see the kind of connection my grandparents had with their extended family. I grew up in the Midwest, but with many southern values. I also have this part of me that is very driven by mission. Not so much career because I will quit a job in a minute if it doesn't align with what I want to accomplish. But I will say mission because everything that enters my life has to make sense to what I have been led to envision for my life. I honestly feel like if I never factored religion and societal moral correctness into my thinking, I would have been much more effective in living out my mission sooner.

I definitely dealt with a bit of shame from being a single mother. I did not deal with that long, though, because when I accepted Christ, I felt like it was really to understand me better, not to be better to find a man or learn the ways of the church so that a good man could desire me. I wanted to understand myself. I only felt like my true creator had those answers. So that shame was gone quickly. Now, some folks tried to make me feel ashamed, but I was in my mid-twenties when I got saved and had a 'child you better gone on now' kind of attitude. Y'all already know how I felt about people by now anyway, so those kinds of shots did not bother me.

There are many things we say we will and will not do before we're in a relationship, and once we are in one, all of that will be challenged. I believe when it comes to marriage, we are a wife or husband before we become one. What I mean by that is that we take on the characteristics before we marry in showing a willingness to serve another person, outside of our desires, so many of us want to be married but show no signs of being a wife or husband before making that commitment. One sign that we might be ready is selflessness. If we have just a bit of selfishness in us, I don't think we are ready. I learned this simply by being in relationships. Two people coming together is not easy.

I think back to trying to understand what Paul in the Bible was saying to the church in 1 Corinthians. I am no Bible scholar, but I know it seemed to me as I was trying to learn to figure myself out, Paul held being single in high regard, not that he looked down on marriage through my interpretation, but as though he saw it as a way that is cultivated to easily distract you from God's mission, but is honored and favored by God. That had an impact on me because I had this mindset that marriage was a principle thing. I mentioned in a previous chapter my battle with this, giving up the idea of marriage and settling, but of course, I tried to pursue it again. Because I held this idea that it's better to be single in the back of my head, if it did not work out, I felt confident that my life would still have a great purpose, even in singleness. Maybe, even more, because I could focus on all the things that were in my heart. I have so many visions of things I desire to accomplish, so being joined in a union was to a degree a hindrance to what I saw for my life, which also made it easier for me to walk away when things were not going how I thought they would.

People who counsel singles will tell them not to feel lonely, while those who counsel couples pursuing marriage will tell them that one reason for marriage is to fulfill loneliness; I've been on both ends, just have yet to actually jump the broom. However, being single with information from both perspectives is very confusing. I feel like if we can just be honest about what we feel, we may be more emotionally healthy in our singleness. To tell single people not to feel lonely suppresses a desire. It's okay to want the things shared in romantic relationships. It's okay to want to be touched, kissed, hugged, listened to, thought of, called on, and I will go as far as to say it's okay to desire sex (I'm not advocating premarital sex!). Religion has done its part in helping to somehow take these things and turn them into something single people should not desire, while society has made it something that single people obsess over, and we have to balance these things out. The best way to do that is to accept that they are a part of us, but they do not have the power to control us.

I can easily turn this into an article to escape my issues dealing with relationships, but I will not do that. I have learned the best part about being single is the right to be selfish in a way. From 2007 to 2010, I decided not to date, just going through self-discovery. Those were really great years for me. It was God and me most nights. I spent time learning to really like myself. I would go to the movies alone. When I could, I would hop in my car late night and take long rides. I would take long walks downtown Chicago. I just spent time loving on myself. I learned to appreciate my strange little figure from my knocked knees to my crooked teeth. I was able to find my sexy in it all and appreciate it without it being defined by society. I discovered the unique things that made me beautiful from the inside out by connecting them to my purpose.

I began thinking about what I enjoyed most as a child. When I got saved, I could say that I felt like a child again. There was so much that I had deposited in my thinking that I had to unlearn, mostly how to have relationships; then, there was so much I had to learn. I was a student at church every Sunday. I observed everything and everyone. I watched how my pastor treated his wife and how she responded to him, along with other couples in leadership positions. I was like a sponge. Prior to this, I never cared to learn because I thought I knew. Of course, with all the good, there was bad, but I had no time to pay those things any attention. As a matter of fact, my years of worldly experience helped me recognize the fools. I hate to say this, but I am going to say it in transparency, I got close to some fools because I knew they did not know any better and would share any and everything. I really wanted to know if I could trust leadership because, being outside of the church, I heard so many rumors about the ills that took place, and a part of me wanted to know so badly that what I was receiving was good because I liked it. I became more and more hopeful the more I learned.

I mentioned I was fifteen when I began dating my son's father. I felt a great deal of responsibility to be loyal to that relationship. I was committed to the idea that we would be together, ultimately, with all the dysfunction we experienced throughout, so young. I can recall, he was gone off to the military, and we were on one of our late-night calls when he asked me if I loved him, and at that time, at that age, I surely did not know what it meant to love someone in a relationship. All I knew was family love. I grew up in a single-parent home, so I had no real example of what woman-to-man love through relationship required. I was hesitant to say that I loved him because I was just unsure. We went back and forth for about 20-minutes on if I loved him or not. Finally, I decided in that short conversation to say yes that I did love him.

In my 16-year-old mind, I was using the information that I had to make that decision. The information that I had was family love. So, when I told him that I loved him, I expected that he would always be supportive, available, and committed just as family is or should be to one another. Although I did not have my father around growing up, I had a great family foundation of support and love, so that is what I knew love to be; togetherness, solid – family. So, this was the expectation that I put on that decision to say that I loved him. I did not know at that age that his learned idea of love was different.

Something being single and dating has taught me is, people, understand common things differently. For example, I thought men looked for wives. I thought a wife was hard-working, intelligent, supportive, beautiful from the inside out, and nurturing. At least, this is what I fixed in my head. Since I was a little girl, I knew I wanted to be a mother, and in order to be a mother, I should probably consider the whole wife thing. So, I enjoyed being that and growing into those attributes. As a single woman, I never expected to be told by men that they could never be with a woman like me or that they'd never marry. Me being who I am would say, oh well! I just would not waste my time with someone who would not consider having the same goals as me. Being who I am, though, I would be lying if I said that those comments did not take a stab at my ego or even what I thought I knew about what men wanted.

Those comments hardened my heart a bit. Of course, I cannot assume that I knew what those guys meant, but in hindsight, it could have been their insecurities or, hell, maybe I just was not the one, obviously now. Then, however, it made me treat men with a heartless approach.

I once read in an article, "Do not mistake desire for love. Desire leaves home in a frantic search for one gratification after another. Love is at home with itself." Although it is normal to desire the things that come along with a relationship, it is crazy to chase after them.

I have learned through experience that we have to be very careful as single people on what we allow to take up residence in our thinking. I have allowed the good old sin, lust, to create fictitious truths in my thinking.

For example, I cannot be the only one who has dated someone and felt like I just knew they were the one. In my thinking, it was okay to have sex with him. I was not lusting after sex, though. I was lusting after a desire to be married. See, lust isn't always seduction or sex. It is ideas too. I told myself, well, this one is going to be my husband anyway, so it's okay to have sex with him, right? WRONG! That's how sin works. It taught me that is why we have to be aware of our weaknesses because once that sin takes root in your weakness, the pain of getting rid of it will feel like having a serious surgery. I can admit that those break-ups felt like the tearing apart of flesh because you've conjoined in something that you should have never joined to begin. It's funny too, because our pride tells us to depart, making the other person feel like they were not good enough. When the truth is, they are good enough for someone else. We sometimes, in our eagerness, place them in a position to be a mate because we are selfish and want to feed that lust desire. We cause them to feel inadequate for being just who they are supposed to be. That is why we cannot be selfish people because doing this and trying to get from people what you want instead of giving what you have created this cesspool of broken singles that I feel like we are experiencing in current times, where the majority of singles are bitter because they never got what they wanted from people instead of focusing on what they are giving to others and being able to weed out those who are undeserving.

At one point in my singleness, after I officially called the roller-coaster relationship with my son's father quits (I stuck around way too long), I allowed that time of frustration to harden my heart. With that, I had gotten even more bitter towards men, then the guys who were predators became my prey. Heartless is what I'd call it. I was flat-out disrespectful. I would entertain the conversation of other men on the phone while I was in the presence of one I was dating. I would pin them against one another because I knew their ego would cause them to compete by asking questions like do you know so-and-so? Then, leave it unaddressed, piquing his curiosity and wondering if so-and-so and I were involved. There were more games I won't expose all of my ills, but I will say, listening to Kanye West's song from the 808's and Heartbreaks "Heartless" made me realize that I was operating that way.

Playing games like this surely isn't the way of a wife, nor is it effective toward the mission of your life. It's the wrong way to handle being single. To get wrapped up in playing games because you are bitter and have not guarded your heart is the mistake so many young people make when they try to find something in a mate that they cannot define for themselves. This is why it is so important to spend time getting to know and understand who you are–designing a plan for your life and learning early to discern God's voice and how He's speaking to you. I don't think we talk about that enough because it sounds weird, but it matters. People speak into your thinking all the time. Like when I said guys would tell me they could never be with a woman like me – I had this conversation with my good friend Kelly. It offended me, but it took me back to what I was saying in chapter one about not being able to move like others. She said, Nia, you're different. She felt they weren't going to even play with me because they knew my expectations were high, and I would hold them to high account. She reminded me that it was a compliment. My friends always tease me for being very smart but slow at catching on to some things. Here she's right because all I heard in those conversations were the rejection.

Now in my late thirties and a mother of two, I am still not clear on what I want as far as ever being married. So many people think I should take into consideration what God wants for me, but I don't see it that way. Just like I do not believe in this idea of "the one," I think God gives us free will to choose in this area. However, I do think He'll give us a glimpse of what's good, or if we crossed a person on our path whose destiny aligns with ours, He will help us recall or think about them because I just genuinely believe God wants to give us the desire of our heart, but ultimately it's up to us. Like even if we saw that person and chose to be single, it would be good in God's eyes. Or we saw that person and chose to marry someone who had a greater need because we felt more compelled to help them that would also be good to God–of course, considering the importance of being equally yoked in the same beliefs and morals.

For me, being single has been rewarding. I feel like a whole complete person without any baggage and plenty of room to become better in other areas like finances and influence. I was at the park with my daughter Lillian on a beautiful day in the Fall, and I was having a conversation with another mother who was there with her kids.

We were just talking about our children and asking what each other did for a living. It was one of those moments like I talked about already. I, at this point, have gotten better at listening and sharing. So, I listened to her, and then I began to share what I worked on and was up to, and as I was talking, I saw her begin to shrink. I saw her also fidgeting with her wedding ring. She was married. It made me realize that we are all so much alike. Married and single women are so much alike. We all just want to walk in our purpose and leave a mark on this earth–our own mark, not through anyone else. Something in our own works that is special and unique, and I believe we all should have that without it being defined by our kids or marriage.

I think a good spouse understands that. I would also listen to conversations with married women. A former colleague told me that she would have never gotten married if she knew what she now knows about marriage. Not that her marriage is in bad shape, many probably make the assumption from that comment, but she and her husband are a great example of what a marriage should look like, in my opinion, but she was referencing the sacrifice it takes. She was saying had she known, it would take that level of sacrifice; she would have waited until she built more for herself or not had married at all. Of course, I cannot speak for married women, but I think most believe that they should be able to have the desires of their hearts and their families to be the healthiest, more grounded version of themselves.

Whether with no kids or with kids, we singles want the same, the healthiest version of ourselves. I believe that we should seek that to be happy and feel fulfilled with life, knowing that it's not that simple. Men and women go through life wondering why we aren't good enough for marriage or why no one wants us, but we are doing what I did to myself with my father, creating a narrative that probably is blocking you from actually getting what you need and desire whether that is wholeness or a mate. In our singleness, everything we do should be to better ourselves, and if you can turn your focus to serving God then, great! But, spending too much time trying to perfect yourself so that you can be chosen is not a good thing because you are not giving them your true authentic self. You should want people to see you as you, who you are authentically, not a made-up version of you to be chosen.

I never felt that a self-love journey was about finding a mate. Instead, I saw it as connecting to a higher being than me. Knowing myself and loving myself had everything to do with who God created me to be. I felt like I had to grab hold of that, or I would destroy and waste my time here on earth. Without connecting spiritually, I felt that a good part of me was missing. All of the other relationships would fail or be unfulfilling without seeing how each and every person was strategically placed on my path to bring me into my fuller, better self. I live my life with the understanding that I am always right where I am supposed to be, but how I interpret that moment has so much to do with my understanding. Either I can progress at that moment or learn a lesson that will help me progress.

This life is a gift; once you learn to live it, breathe in it, and accept things as they are when they show up, you slowly begin to release the trauma, fear, and all the extra baggage. Just being may sound scary to some people, possibly because they have not traveled through their self-love journey, getting in touch with God and a deeper level of understanding yourself and purpose once you put the fear of what you might find aside and go for it; It's worth it to be free. When people say they are free, I always think to myself, at what cost, because I know I had to let go of a lot of shit to get here. I am still gaining mental, emotional, and psychological freedom every day until I am truly free in Heaven.

Self-Evaluation

Please journal your answers on the empty pages provided at the end of the chapter.

1. What is my purpose?
2. What is my vision for my life?
3. Am I a selfless person?

What is my Purpose: Understanding my purpose helped me make sense of so many things and also helped me shape what I would bring to a marriage and desire to get out of one. I think this work of discovering your purpose is necessary before marriage. It may take some time. You may start thinking about your purpose as a child, with understanding your gifted areas and how you can apply them in life, but it's in those young adult years when you get out into the world and learn about the issues of the world and how what you know can help fix problems. That is when you can think about what good you can do for society.

What is my vision for my life: I remember being asked this in a premarital class. At that point, I was solid on what I wanted. I knew and was working on it. Marriage should reflect that vision you have for your life. A marriage, I think, should be colliding visions of you and your mate that give a foundation to your marriage. They say, what do you bring to the table all the time, I say you both should meet at the table to bring the vision that you both have for your life, and that table should cultivate the plan that you have for the marriage. Many may say that sounds like a business, but it's the business of the institution you are building that will be honored by God. I feel like the marriage should have a mission that two people should be working toward. Yes, you get distracted from that mission in catering to each other, but you return to focus on that plan. If I don't have that, what is the point of having a marriage? In my eyes, marriage starts with one having a vision for their own life. This will show your mate that you are a good person to partner with because you plan things out, envision your life to prepare for things you desire. I did not require any of this in my previous relationships, but I wish I would have. We have to move beyond just wanting to get married because our parents weren't or were, or because we feel it's the moral thing to do.

Am I a selfless person: I feel like I have always been very selfless. The first time I spent I shutting out the idea of a relationship and dating, was so rewarding because I occupied myself with things I desired. Even at 16 years old, I was thinking about someone else's heart desires and taking that into consideration to factor into my dreams. Being single does not necessarily mean that you are selfish with a lack of compassion for others, though. We can find time to serve in so many ways and giving to others no matter the form is always rewarding, but I know desiring a marriage requires two selfless people always finding the time and ways to serve each other. In my mind, that is the only way I see marriage.

Dealing with a Perfectionist Attitude

Reference Matthew 11:28-30 - He doesn't want you striving so hard to achieve, all on your own. He wants to provide you rest. You don't need to carry a heavy burden by yourself; Jesus will help you carry it. He will do the heavy lifting for you, so you aren't weighed down by the pursuit of perfection.

Chapter 5

I can remember always being called anal. Every time I enter into a new situation or environment, I set the standard of expectations very high. I have a very high work ethic, which is important, and much of the time, I hold people to the same high standard that I set for myself. The problem with that is I will not set the standard so that I may achieve it within a reasonable amount of time. I have learned that issues like perfectionism is directly connected to trauma.

I've done this with relationships, my business, and even ministry. I am quite sure it's spilled over into my parenting, probably more in that area than any, because we all want to be good parents and do not want our children to make some of the same mistakes that we have.

Sometimes, even if you do not have the characteristics of a perfectionist, you may find yourself being obsessive with your child(ren). For example, I can remember my poor baby boy when he started preschool and came home with his first homework assignment. He had been in school for a few weeks already, and I knew I had done my job as a parent, teaching him the things he needed to know to prepare him. So, I picked him up from my aunt's house, which was where he went once school let out while I was commuting from work, then we headed home. When I got home, I went through his backpack, looking for a note from the teacher as I always would, and there was a worksheet and on it read, "HOMEWORK." I thought it was pretty cool because my son's learning process in life through formal education was beginning. So, we ate dinner, played for a little while; I mean, he was only three or four years old, then I sat him down at the table to do the worksheet.

It started fine, but as we were identifying the alphabets, he drew a blank. It angered me beyond belief because, at that moment, I could not understand how we've spent so much time going over this, and I know they've been going over the same thing in preschool because I saw the work that he brought home.

Anxiety hit me, and I panicked. In my head, I thought that something might be wrong with my son; I could not imagine how he could not remember these things. So I turned militant on him and began yelling at my child, attempting to force him to recall what I knew he had known.

Suddenly, I grabbed hold of myself when I looked at the fear in his eyes and the tears welling up, I felt horrible, but since I was stuck on committing, I did not stop fussing at him as I walked away. I went into the bathroom and had a moment of trying to figure out what was happening to me. Finally, I calmed down and went back out. Once I calmed down, he began to recall what he knew, and I began to celebrate him, and we went on with our night until bedtime.

I could not rest well that night as I recalled my behavior; I felt horrible. I did not know if I had scarred my son for life. I did not feel good about what I had done, and over time I became more and more conscious of these kinds of outbursts, typically when things were not going my way.

Sometimes, we have to check the kid in us. At heart, we're all that little person, and that is an okay thing, but we apply it in areas we are supposed to be mature instead of going before God child-like when we need him to carry us through. When we do not confront our own bad behaviors like anything else that's fed, it grows. In my case, I fed that perfectionists attitude with my mild accomplishments or the expectations that others had for me.

Perfectionism is probably the most detrimental thing to creativity that exists. I know that I went through feeling like I had to present myself in a way that made me seem perfect. I realized that had everything to do with me being insecure, not 100% sure of myself and doubting my abilities, not feeling like I was capable of accomplishing the things that I desired to do. Perfectionism clouded my thinking and forced me to become someone I was not.

I became stubbornly focused on the professional persona. I did not desire to be a stay-at-home mother. I wanted it all. A mission-driven career, and I was committed to that - achieving it all was my tunnel-visioned focus. I may have gotten lost in the idea of having it all at times. I would try to move with perfection, all the while making every mistake and not even noticing it because my focus was on the outcome and not the process. Growing up Black in America, we can see other successful Black people, but we don't get to see a lot of the process to success; much of the time, we only get to see the outcome.

Eventually, I had to let go of perfectionism and lean into a sense of compassion for others, and that is where I found I had a purpose in life. My destiny was attached to my legacy. So I had to let perfectionism go – that perfectionism was my Achilles heel.

There are so many things that we deal with as women - especially when it comes to this idea of work/life balance if there's a such thing. Relinquishing this idea of being perfect was the one for me. In being trapped in that thinking, what I was putting out was not at all what I was trying to cultivate for my life. I may have begun to come off to people as a snob when I was reaching for success in reality. Actually, caught in two worlds because my crew of friends is some of the most down-to-earth people I know. It was those down-to-earth people that would hold up a mirror at times so that I could see myself for what I was giving out. They still cared about me, but they would say things in innuendos that let me know I was tripping. Those are good friends, I would say.

People, especially young Black women, have this strange battle – men may have it too, but women especially. We get opportunities to grow in corporate America, and it takes a toll and has an influence on us. It's being in this strange world that White men dominate. We have to spend time evaluating what we are willing to sacrifice to go down that path. For me, I loved my people. I never wanted to be too good to go to the hood and have a cocktail with my friends or just hang out with people I came up with. I think this is an internal battle when choosing to be successful. The mindset that we have to let go to move up is a choice I never really wanted to make. No one has ever told me that I had to make that choice, but it's apparent when friendships begin to grow apart because I was changing. At some point, those people that would call me out for acting "90210ish" were not around anymore, but I felt I had to keep that level-headedness without putting on this façade of perfection and beating myself up for making bad decisions along the way.

I had to grow up and learn to encounter people who would tell me things that I was wrong about; in order for me to realize, at some point, that it is important in growth to remain teachable. I think many of us in our twenties, for some reason, have the personality that I talked about at the beginning of the book. I think many of us in our twenties go through an I know it all phase, and no one can tell us anything. We think we have the answers to everything. But, what's funny is by the end of your twenties, something happens, God gives a gift. I don't know if it happens for everyone, but for those of us hard-headed ones, it definitely happens. Well, I call it a gift because what it does is set you straight to let you know that you don't have the answers and you're not going to always get it right. My gifts came in the form of relationships. I thought that I could orchestrate relationships the way I wanted them to be because, to me, I was perfect. I knew what I wanted, and I knew how to achieve it.

The dismantling of those relationships is really what helped me realize I can't dictate to my life. Everything is not going to go the way that I want them to go.
Life doesn't work like that. Especially being in Christ, I

really had to allow God to direct my path. If I trust God, if I believed the way I wanted to, I had to be teachable because the people that He guides you to on your path are there for you to get something from them; we are all vessels, usable vessels, and I believe that.

The Application of Learning to be Teachable

I wanted to change my ways, you all know how that is – with one change, you want everything to change immediately. In my early twenties, I was working as a contract employee, but before that, I had spent years in banking. In my thinking, working for the association, I was positioning myself for my future. That know-it-all in me had to do everything right and according to my order. I wanted when I graduated to be in a position to do things the way I thought that I should. That meant making money to provide for myself and my son.

I was working this job, and I thought I was doing the right thing. However, I did not feel like I was in the right place or in the right position. So, I decided to let go of that contract job, and I went back to banking. I spent years working at various banks, starting when I was 17 years old. I decided to go back; this was when I thought I would get into regional marketing using my journalism degree. So, I went back to the bank that I worked for before working for the association as a contract employee. Probably three months after being back, something was tugging me to go back to the association.

I eventually did, but so many people in the door were telling me to be careful; they would tell me about the Director, who was a lot like myself, somewhat of a perfectionist. So, once I realized that, I didn't worry about it because I had already trained myself to deal with that kind of pressure that comes from a perfectionist's attitude, although I was getting better at this point in my life.

August of 2008, I had my first day on the job. I will never forget I asked her a question about something administrative and she said to me, can't you do everything? Now my favorite movie is "Devil Wears Prada," and I immediately thought, oh, she's an Miranda Priestly type. So at that point, I knew exactly what I was dealing with.

I also knew that this would be a test for me. I knew it would be a test because I began to understand that I needed to learn how to humble myself. I was at a place in my life where I just thought everything had to be a certain way. I never considered various avenues, so being in a position allowing me to begin to humble myself was good for me. I say that because I had to submit to her authority, I had to finish it out, even though I would typically quit a job in a second. But, there was a way for me to become a better person for my journey.

I know people don't like that, to say submitting to someone's authority. Anytime you use the word submit, it is like WHOA, but I had to learn to submit to authority so that I can hear instruction. So that I could remain teachable throughout my life when I was in my twenties, I just couldn't hear. I knew what I wanted, and, in my eyes, I knew how to get there and how to get there was having a worker's mentality. I thought I could work my way into success. By having this worker's mentality, I didn't care how many jobs I had to work. I didn't care what job I had to do; I just wanted to make money.

I began to break that mentality in this role because I had to submit to that authority, and there were times I struggled mentally immensely in having a moment where I had to do something that I just didn't want to do. I just didn't feel as though some of the administrative tasks were right for me when I had my degree; At this point, I was gaining confidence in myself in feeling like I knew what I wanted out of life. When I began to feel that, it was when the challenge came. I had to clear some files out of a file cabinet, organizing files that were in a file cabinet. It infuriated me so badly because I'm happy doing what I was expected to do with my regular job requirements. This new task reminded me of the contract role that I left. I was a records clerk, then having to do other things like her keeping my phone ringing constantly to ask questions about her calendar and phone list as if I were a personal assistant got the best of me, and I had to go in the bathroom and breakdown and pray. I told God; I get this is my assignment. I get I have to do this, but I need you to help me! I learned at that moment that I don't have to be perfect, and to go before God for His strength. I can go forward guided by His instructions. That was so liberating for me because when you are someone who thrives on getting it right all the time, you realize that you run into so many brick walls. Constantly doing that puts you in this constant state of feeling defeated because everything seems to go wrong. When you're pursuing your dreams and your passion, and you're trying to get in proper alignment with who you are supposed to be, you're going to meet challenges. This is why I can appreciate that role and that woman because it was able to break that spirit of wanting to win at everything.

I learned in that experience what servitude is really about and how submitting to authority can benefit you as long as you stay in prayer and know when to ask God for direction. I had to submit to authority; I learned my imperfections are something that can be hindering but can also be a blessing in leaving room for me to grow and know better. My imperfection was trying to be perfect and being hard on myself when I could not manifest that perfection.

That is not only exhausting; it can impact your mental health, creating a fear of failure causing anxiety and depression. That role repositioned my thinking about my path, and I think I was able to see that because I was open to learning the lesson. I felt so confident about moving into entrepreneurship at this point.

As I mentioned before, I learned what I needed there

and gained more knowledge for my own path, on gaining insight in seeking funding. God used that woman to lead me to where I am supposed to be. I left that company, and I was not angry or bitter, but my next level for the next step in my life, I was equipped with more tools.

I still struggled with fear of failure a bit, especially in the early days of building my company, but I did not try so hard to be perfect and learned in some ways to embrace failure. It's all a process and journey. When you begin to love yourself more, the more you desire to free yourself from tormenting habits, like being too hard on yourself and beating yourself up for things you really cannot control.

Self-evaluation:

Please journal your answers on the empty pages provided at the end of the chapter.

1. Identify your bad habit that hinders your growth?
2. What do you need to address specifically to fix it?

Identify your bad habit that hinders your growth: For me, as I explained throughout the chapter, it was using perfectionism to beat me up throughout my younger years. This constant desire to get everything right so that I would not look like a failure, even though I was failing, mostly myself on having good healthy experiences in life. I learned nothing I tried to do that "looked" perfect works.

What do you need to address specifically to fix it: I am not sure if you caught this in the chapter, but the very specific thing that I needed to address was compassion. In acquiring this perfectionist's attitude to appeal to this corporate world, I began to lose sensitivity to the world around me and was becoming cold and only thinking about achieving success for myself. Not my community or legacy, even though I would convince myself that climbing would be for my legacy. I realized in gaining humility that was a lie. Fixing that changes the trajectory completely. God gave me that.

"You alone are enough," Dr. Maya Angelou

Chapter Six: Closing Remarks

The wonderful late mother, Dr. Maya Angelou, is often quoted as saying that "you alone are enough."

Back in 2016, I was pregnant with my 2nd child, my little girl. While I was pregnant, I was in law school, completing a master's degree in intellectual property. Before I got pregnant, in late 2015, I was in my entertainment law class, the professor mentioned how great Sundance was and how it was a great place to network, so I planned to go. Fast Forward Winter 2016, I was pregnant in the mountains at Sundance Film Festival. No clue on what to do, who to mingle with, and the professor that mentioned the place greatness left me hanging no call, no plans to meet, nothing after contacting him and him agreeing to meet up. So, I just went on enjoying my trip. I saw some great films and engaged in an interesting dialogue with natives and festival-goers, not to mention my frightening trips going up and down the mountains while it was snowing to get to my hotel and the festival. For most of the trip, I was ALONE; one of my good friends did come to join me for a day but had to return home.

For many of us, we find it hard to go out and do things ALONE. We think we have to have a partner in crime for everything. We buy two tickets to an event without even knowing who's going with us. We stay home because we don't have someone to commit to hanging out with us. We won't do things like buy a house, think about having kids through fostering or adopting (if you're not a single parent already), or opening our own businesses; we do not take those international vacations, start a new church because we are concerned about when are WE going to get the partner to do all these things with us. But YOU ALONE ARE ENOUGH! As single parents, we fail to make moves that bring attention to us out of fear that this imaginary microscope will bring our truth to judgment, so we live small, waiting to get someone by our side to silence the judgment. Sometimes, we won't take our children to church out of the fear we'll be judged. We won't brag about our kids in professional environments like the married people because we know at their mention eyes will look down to our hands in search of the symbol of moral correctness. So we live silent; we live meekly, we live isolated, waiting for someone to come along to be the person that makes us whole, but YOU ALONE ARE ENOUGH!

I know because, to pursue my own dreams, I had to be enough, alone. I mentioned I went to Sundance Film Festival; I planned the trip with no partner in mind. My friend planned her flight after mine was booked. My companion at the time was like, are you sure? And I was like YEP! Because I learned from being single that I alone am in charge of my destiny, just as you are in charge of yours.

Journey of Your Life

When I began writing this memoir, I knew there were going to be some things about me that I would have to face. I got a lot of it out, but there were areas that I was still dealing with that I needed time to separate myself from to begin elaborating on them in writing. I mean, a memoir is recounting your journey. There's a reflection in that, evaluation, and correction. But I completed it. In 2010, I left my job to start my publishing company, where I have a magazine, and I train up young writers while attempting to continue efforts to uplift people in our communities. I completed my law degree and began a career in communications. Its been an upward climb, but it has not been easy. I have been broke, judged, turned on by people I KNEW had my back; it made absolutely no sense for them not to have my back. I looked for work for at least 8-years seriously and got no's for eight years. While growing my business, trying to shape relationships for marriage, reshaping my career, trying to be a homeowner. I failed at it all. All those no's while carrying the burden of judgment for being a single mother.

The silent burden of judgment. No one outright says it, but I was told when I finished teacher's training at my church and began teaching young adults, one of the other teachers that was an older woman, asked, why don't I start a single mother class? I responded, maybe I will, but I had to learn here; first, she later stopped teaching, and ironically the woman that took her place was another single mother (laughs).

I was still going through life, but teaching there taught me that I would have to be bold. I showed up every Sunday ready to teach a lesson about the love of Christ Jesus and His unmerited favor and His forgiveness, and the more I taught, the more the lessons emboldened me. Now, had I listened to that woman and tried to create something pre-maturely, I would not have received the keys that I needed to pursue my mission. Under-handed insult can be something else when it touches a tender spot, but you have to know that YOU ALONE ARE ENOUGH.

Back then, I may have known that, but I felt it; God was cultivating my understanding that I alone am enough.

When he sat me down in those mountains to watch that Maya Angelou film, maybe two years later is where he confirmed it.

Many of us women clothe ourselves in the facade of toughness and strength in an effort to guard our hearts, but true strength, real strength, boldness, and courage you cannot see. You have to have a real encounter with a person to know it's there. You don't know what I've endured just by looking at me. It's true! I've gotten into relationships with men, and they, for some reason, think that my kindness is a sign of weakness, and they have attempted to play the games and play on a naivety, that's when they realize that true kindness is not a weakness it's a strength because you can exude truth in being kind you have a worth to protect. Your tolerance for games is low, your non-negotiables, and your standards are high.

I talk about all this in my book, coming into those understandings. Understanding my worth and beginning to know the root of self-love is knowing and being in a relationship with God, the Father. I think this book is a good opportunity for us to peel back the layers and begin to expose who we truly are; Black people, specifically, we are amazing people. If you ask God to lend you a pair of spiritual eyes to see how he sees us, you'll see each one of us matter to the big picture. That's why Alone you are enough because you're a part of this huge puzzle, and without you realizing that, we'll never complete the puzzle, so we need you. Our community needs you. The world needs you!!! Get the book, do your work, pull back the layers, and talk to God as you do it. Cry, scream, take breaks to go through your story, mend broken pieces, and make sense of pained areas but at the end, you are healed, and a healed individual helps heal a broken society.

Author Q & A

Why did you title your book "As Thyself?"

It's from the Bible verse, "Love Thy Neighbor As Thyself." I've heard so many sermons, read many articles and lessons on Love Thy Neighbor, but I wanted to find a way to focus on self-love. I wanted to explore that understanding from a biblical position. "Love thy neighbor as thyself" was Jesus' second command and we always hear it I think with others in mind, but I think it included the ability to love yourself as well as others.

What made you want to write a book about self-love?

I had to get there. I had to get to a place where I loved everything about me. Not that I was taught not to love myself. I was just shaped by so many experiences and most of those experiences came from making moves with bad information, so I had to dig deep to find out what I learned wrong to remove it, what I learned properly to enhance it, and what I did not learn at all to learn it. That all started with learning who God created me to be.

How did you decide which stories to share from your experiences?

The ones that had the most impact. The ones that caused me to dig and evaluate. I'm not that old so most of the stories happened in my 20's and they stemmed from childhood brokenness and I was able to connect the experiences to the buried hurt.

How long have you been a writer?

All my life. I was born to do this. I'm still growing as a storyteller, but I can remember being very small and sitting against a closed bedroom door escaping by writing in my mickey mouse journal. I've always been able to express my thoughts better through written word. There's a joy I cannot get from anything else like when I write. Excitement, eagerness, happiness, imagination, and recollection all hit me at once. It's a great feeling.

When did you discover you were a good writer?

I don't think that I am "good" I feel like I'm okay and growing. I recall two moments when I knew I was really called to do this. Once, in sixth grade when the teacher would always use my papers as examples to the class, then again my senior year in high school when the teacher read my paper aloud calling it perfect. After that I knew it would be a long journey to me becoming a great writer, but I believe I am on my way.

What have you had published prior to this book?

I have two guide books "Shattered by Violence; Mended by God," an administrative guide, but mostly articles. I have spent years working on my craft and cultivating my thoughts and plans, so I started my magazine. I never wanted a big company to benefit from my hard work and debt accumulated from investing in my higher education. Nor, have I wanted to water down my message. So, i've written freelance for a few publications, but I am most proud of the articles I have written for my own publication, because I wrote from my heart in my truth. I can recall writing an article about celibacy, but it was really about choosing to abstain, but the publisher did not have a full understanding of what celibacy is and the commitment it required. I wrote the article from the perspective of the publisher, but it still bothers me because I feel like I failed in truly educating people when I knew better. That's one article, I could not imagine feeling that way with an entire portfolio of work. I have few, but I'm proud of my work, because it's me, my truths and transparency.

Is that why you decided to self-publish?

Absolutely. I could not see it any other way. I don't likebeing lied to or told someone is capable of doing something for my dreams that I cannot do for myself. Don't get me wrong, I'm fine being taught or mentored, but I don't believe in other people controlling my vision. I understand some people don't have time, so they need publishers, but I decided to make time, because I am tied to the entire idea of writing and publishing is the biggest part, so I wanted to master that part for myself.

Will there be another book?

Ehhhh...I don't know yet. I really want to spend some time focusing on my magazine and making it a community go to publication for a source of impartation on current cultural spirituality through accounts of everyday people. We are suppose to be living epistles I want to capture that. I started a piece about a prostitute in the magazine, so I might turn that into a fiction novel, but I haven't decided yet.

Acknowledgements

My parents, I am so grateful for what they have given me to become the whole woman that I am today. Especially, my mother, in my adult years she has been so supportive in allowing me to become a whole human. God could not have given me a better mother.

My Auntie JoAnn Jones (2017), auntie gave me a moment during a breakdown. I felt defeated, and I was on the floor crying and she walked in the room and said, "Nia, I saw you in a vision on a stage, like at the "Black Girls Rock" she always did that was right on time with words of encouragement.

My Kids, Daniel and Lillian, they hold up a mirror everyday to show me who I am and that helps me become a better person everyday. My soul needed these kids they are true gifts from God.

My Jones family, I love you all beyond words, you are the example of a village the world needs see. I hope we can get that back as we continue to grow our families.

Last, but not least, my brother, Charan – I always hear you brother, always!

www.ingramcontent.com/pod-product-compliance
Lightning Source LLC
Chambersburg PA
CBHW070624120726
47909CB00004B/1307

* 9 7 8 0 6 9 2 2 9 8 0 6 0 *